Noctivagation

Noctivagation

CHEN JUFEI

NOCTIVAGATION

iUniverse books may be ordered through booksellers or by contacting:

iUniverse
1663 Liberty Drive
Bloomington, IN 47403
www.iuniverse.com
844-349-9409

ISBN: 978-1-6632-4410-9 (sc)
ISBN: 978-1-6632-4418-5 (e)

Print information available on the last page.

iUniverse rev. date: 08/31/2022

Contents

1. *Stocks*

A puppet escapes from his master,
Washing the birthmarks off his face，born of fire.
A scholar experienced a catastrophe，curtly,
Entrusting his alimony and lung to a derusting-worker.

A horse suddenly sprang out of his body,
Letting his plan fall through completely.
The falling rain suddenly stopped,
Proving that the weather forecast a failure.

2. Spring-Tides Occur with The Rain

Man with an umbrella decorates the spring
Unfolding it automatically for it's raining-
And springs pop out like the words burst out.
He needs to erect
The crossroad – on his back,
There's indeed a burden to carry.

Since a wound-up oriole began to sing,
He has to follow the birdsong, embedded within
A man with a black umbrella.
He has to seek the fate of the ferry
To turn the umbrella upside down freely
– As the ship is in the hands of eternity.
Alongside the stream grass lies waste.

★Confucius signed by the river and Heraclitus—
washed his feet on the other side.
The edge of the sky is suitable for empty space,
stray people say the same crap.
A tide counts the past; A gust of wind blows,
blowing the oilpaper umbrella away from the boatman's hands.

★Confucius, an important Chinese ancient philosopher, once
said before the river: "The passage of time is just like the flow
of water, which goes on and on, regardless of day and night."
While Heraclitus, an ancient Greek philosopher, once
expressed the same idea: "One can't step into the same river
twice."

3. *Chopsticks in The Pure Water*

Chopsticks reach the taste buds
Like two small bridges.
When they stand respectfully in the bowl,
They become a Buddha,
Water clothes it with cassock. Then
Starry night and moths rubbing against cobwebs,
As if nobody has been offended.

It's like calling another dimension.
— This slender cell phone, tried to dial
The gods' number.
Sometimes, chopsticks defy the gravity,
Popping off to deliver an urgent email.
And sometimes fail as a fallen temple

Let mothers renew with devotion, lift up
The heavy sigh of life.
But the line was still unconnected-
Weak signal, flickering lights.
People having a fever
See the chopsticks returning
To the bamboo one by one,
Returning to empty light flesh.

*Author's note: Using chopsticks for divination is an ancient
Chinese superstition. It is used to bring back the lost souls of
the living and make them heal when a patient is in a coma

4. *A Poem of Mid-age*

A little flame, sitting in the wood. A bundle of sticks,
Cut down from the mountains; decay becomes
A kind of practice. And what does the practice mean?
Accordingly, after my middle age,
Flame repairs the chimney,
And smoke wire-walking in the air, cure for the fear of heights.

Walking in the night, your chest
Makes a bobbing sound — a long time ago, you had
gulp down a sea.
So much salt, you could not help coughing —
Tears bursting out by the fire pan.
To the mirror, I saw the salt grains turning into white flower.

Next door, the lion faster asleep, daughter
Is playing the piano. The snow has not fallen as the forecast reports,
The axe is rusted and a fungus grows
on its handle.
"Bring an unrelated man to earth,
And listen to the avalanche inside it." ★

★ Quoted from Hu Xian's poem.

5. *Noctivagation*

The breeze sends the invitation, the moon seals the postmark.
Shadow, my guest
Not yet — ginkgo's top
Came into a cloud, and this swab is big enough,
Enough to reach down the throat of the vault of heaven.
The lake is bright, issuing a test sheet.

Shadows have feminine beauty. It's like
An idle woman awake —
When the lights are out, insects breaks the walls,
And I'm facing the wall,
Shadows in between, facing the flow of time,
It always has the right to be silent.

Stepping into the atrium is different. When the guests arrived,
Do the shadow and I get together?
I accept the moonlight scanning over me,
Shadow, against a wall, as if
The wall is empty, like a rippling banana-plant,
To be something recognizable in a reversed world.

6. *Watch The Sunset by The Window*

-After reading biography of Wang Anshi★

The wuthering pines are playing the harp of the clouds. In
the dreams,
Wind's fingers, capture a dragon.
Before their nap, one of them is a friend,
The other is an enemy. Now,
One tower is under construction. The tower of pine cones,
Are more stable than the Green Seedling Law★.

Another is praying for rain, trying to make spring
Developed and time keeps the negative.
"It's on the lantern festival, sunny. I'm writing
Symphony — in the second movement,
Mixed with a few drops of birdsong, as a gift.
And the mountains will pay for the sunset."

Anyone can be an audience.
A pine needle pricked a snake's gall, during the concert.
The coir raincoat in the corner, still remembers the weather.
Water logging is in a part of the rain
Where it stops — as the magma cools,
The stone is already in play.

★Wang Anshi: statesman, writer, thinker and reformer of The Northern Song Dynasty of China。

★The Green Seedling Law, also known as the "New Law of Changping", was one of the measures of Wang Anshi's reform in The Song Dynasty of China.

7. *Spiders in Lvov*

— To Adam Zagajewski

How to understand it — A spider is born in a broken web,
And the thick silk which it spews.
To praise, or to repair the world?
Now, a spider hangs over the towering church.
It will be forgotten when it talks about where its belong.
And in the bright night, the moonlight renews its passport.

Some were baptizing plants, others, going to sleep
On the Poetry Day. The moth breaks the web,
Exile for love. "Search for the radiance,
But don't neglect the darkness. "Yes,
Lvov still exists. And now it's spring,
The breeze is real, blowing the town after the the COVID.

"I'll never see you again," just like that
We never met. Would I be in a twilight
Writing a Polish poem, on a winter day?
The cobwebs in the barracks are like moonlight,
This metaphor of failure tempts me go to Lvov
Which exists, after all, quiet and pure like a peach tree.

8. *A River*

Twilight lines up for seating to test
The temperature of the water. The sunset glow lights it up.
Every spray hides a secret.
As the breeze thumbs through the sorghum field,
People are tipsy and real.

Autistic suffer burst his words out.
No sooner had he pulled himself out of the wine glasses
Than he plunged into the streamers fermented by the solid
pendulum.
At that time, the stars were all over the sky, Just one more
drink,
Instantly, one could have the flesh of the universe.

The Big Dipper ticks the sky, while the porcelain temple
Seals the memorial tablet for grains.
Some sniff the spring wine, some pour a glass of dark blue,
Some come knocking and leave the world hanging
An island inhabited by sages. At that time
The river is as clear as jade, time gives off a rich aroma.

9. *Tallow Tree in The Snow*

The New Year falls on the old snow. Wind, is a verb.
Make belfry cough every once in a while,
The people downstairs, their inner world
Were coated in wax. In the fall,
He had set himself on fire, and now he suddenly woke up
From the dream: a pair of footprints disappeared —

It's like suspense. On the overpass, snow is gathering,
To pass chalks to teachers. It's willing to
Devote the rest of his life to a blank sheet of paper. so
Very good. When he finishes his letter, he will inset the quill
Into a porcelain vase. Wuhu Road
Is a long letter, as night falls, lamps is coming to read it.

Best wishes. Memories can be transplanted,
He remembered the old moors, Punctuation marks
Like crows, scattered in piles of clouds,
He envied the blackbirds, the snowflakes,
Who shook furry wings and cause words
An avalanche...

10. *A Town*

When I returned from overtime work, I sometimes saw
The autumn wind riding a tiger★.
Jump into Chaohu Lake.
Time to back to the nest, the moon pours silvery stream
down, in the sky
The last bowl is empty and round.
Sometimes I hear the sycamore playing the organ,
In my ears, the flame dances, in time.

Countlessly, wake from dreams. outside the window.
Mournful music, is lower than the sound of a tick.
Haven't been home for a long time, fallen leaves,
Help comfort your dead father.
Pick out the thorns in your hands, with pine needles.
Picking, picking, then dawn breaks, like the blood gushed out.

A tree does not remember its own craft.
Last night, it played an unknown tune,
Accidentally saved a loved one from a tiger's paws.
Morning, the streets opened it narrow gates. The vegetables
are fresh,
The buyer was still yawning
The sun is broken and dappled, revealing animal tattoos.

★This is a Chinese term of idiom referring to very hot
weather which occurs in autumn.

11. *Wind Line*

The chess game in the sky is over. East of the city
Cough first, like in the throat, live
A man who sings Laosheng★. And on the roof,
Snow sings the white face★. In the dream,
The astrologer, wearing a mask, agreed.
And tomorrow he'll be wearing a tighter mask.

The camphor tree hides a violin.
Chemical plants put down their butcher knives and practice
like old monks.
On the gate, a Chinese character reported it.
Those who ran as fast as they could to the platform,
Wallowing in a mountain temple, taking revenge, and finally,
Dumped by the ski resort again.

The car said the past, outside the car,
The morning exerciser sings the opera. Black people
Looks blacker in the snow today.
Last night's horoscope did not include these.
Quantum bursts, the universe is chaotic,
After a breeze, the snowman went to work.

★Laosheng (opera trade) also known as Xu Sheng, Sheng,
or beard. Laosheng mainly plays male roles above middle
age, singing and chanting with his own voice (true voice)
Laosheng basically wears three dreadlocks of black beard,
the term is called "black three".

★"Red face" and "white face" are derived from Peking Opera
facial makeup, in which loyal officials or good people are red
face and treacherous officials or bad people are white face.

12. *Mobile Museum*

The gear turns the calendar. The calendar, renewing the days,
Make other things old.
I have a mobile museum, and years ago,
I built it up during the evening of rush hour.
Inns, suspended in the air like lonely islands —
It has intangible lifting power.

Do flowers stir up a storm? I have to bear
The acceleration of the festival. Otherwise,
It was a success. While adding a reflection, it's a failure.
The bell tower patted the startled wood,
In an instant, the white clouds were solemn, and sunshine
was silent: A drummer passed under a paulownia.

Only at night — compared to
The shadows of the day, the light is impossible to hide.
I showed it my collection:
Except for a few drops of water, and
Footprints in the snow. I used some of them
Redeemed spring.

13. *Rulers*

The ruler has clear scale. When
Something has to be given up,
Replace it with a proper one. Then,
It holds the power of life and death.
The spring is raging. The crowd is rushing.
Both are dodging rulers hanging over their heads.

Sunshine measures shadow with ginkgo's ruler.
Noon comes. Shadow
Is getting shorter and shorter. Ginkgo, however,
Provides the data with accurate records.
A glass of water can also measure the sea—
It's clear, thirst-quenching, and dreams of billowing waves.

Clock measures time, as disease measures life.
Death took away my father, using
Some rulers. After several measurements,
My father accepted the rulers of the other world.
And I was left with the word "father,"
As a ruler to test me.

14. *Nanguan River*

Maiden was taking photos with Beauty Cam, an old man
Participated in composition, eating pickled shrimp,
Smelled like a feeling of life. Firework sellers swung wooden boats
From far away, to eat pickled shrimp.
This scene, exists or not?
The stone bridge said yes, but maples and aspens said no.

How long ago was the Song Dynasty? History is shaking in the river.
Oars, are poking the phantom of a postbox,
At the gate of Dongyue Temple, people holding oars are still watching a play.
That was in the live video
Memories can recapture absent boats
In front of a camera, to show the craft of crossing the universe of time.

The autumn wind, like a postman, posts a letter from white clouds
to the river bottom. Oiled paper umbrella reflects in the river, upside down,
The past and the future are symmetrical along the realistic eaves.
Including the white clouds,
Everything can reserve.
Everything can be folded except the wind of autumn.

15. *Late-Night Conversation at Manshan Island*

The lake is ebbing. This is obvious–
When I call out to the lake,
The stars seem to swell.
Whitefish leaps on either side of Pegasus
In the invisible silence. The cogongrass are shaking,
The lighthouse is holding up, and we begin to argue from
now on.

"Was it a misanthrope or Someone who loved life that the
first to come?"
For a second, we thought we heard
The sound of persimmons falling. Sometimes,
An island is better than an empire.
Picking up chestnut, It's better to collect chestnuts shells.

The girl next to me got stabbed,
Which reminded us that the night consisted of
A lot of light made of thorns. When we
Got lost, the flashlight opened the acupoint of a path.
We said goodbye to her at the dock in the morning,
The silver needles billowed and the spray was like herbs.

16. *For Tea*

Dack clouds hang heavily before the rain. From halfway up the mountain,
A dragon springs from a stream,
To test the temperature of the new fire. Who is the most familiar
With the art of slaying dragons?
Slutty lady A, her arm rose and the sword fell. Carl B,
Boil spring and autumn in an iron cast pot.

White clouds wing softly, after the rain, Upon which the cranes' nests perhaps be
Surprisely, the birthplace of the poems of Chu is here.
When the spring swallow returns to its nest, the mud it carries,
Is also my home land.
Village boy C, with red paint on his brow,
Is responsible for highlight the eyes of the dragon boat, after drinking up half a cup of tea.

The teapot of heaven and earth is so big.
A tea tree, enlightened before an orchid.
Devote it's life, and then,
Relife in a porcelain cup. A villager as me,
Drinking the mist and the stream and the heat of time,
Reject internal roll and get a simple stretch.

17. *Qingyang Tune*

What can stop a mother from aging?
If, she has been living in Qingyang tune.
An apricot wooden case for a wedding
Can back to an almond tree with green fruit.
But now, apricot flowers are in bloom
At the top of the mother's head. Like a white cloud,

On the top of Jiuhua Mountain. On the stage,
It's singing "Roll," with drums and cymbals.
The sound of cracked stones from the clouds
Pour down into the world. The crowd looking up,
Accept the unbearable weight.
Mother shed muddy tears as if,

Meteorites weigh less than apricot flowers. As if,
The acidity of the green apricot is finally released.
Her life is soaked in the old wooden box.
After the show, the ring of fire extinguished, mountain wind
Blew through the silent black hole, emptied the boom,
Only the lonely moon, was hanging as a lamp.

18. *Travel Notes of Taiping Mountain House*

The bees, are carrying their motherland.
Sunshine is the most precious to export.
All the taxes have been reduced,
A stone plaque records the event.
Under the clear sky, the sun gives more subsidies
To roofs and the rape fields.

Conversely, at night, it is the same —
The carp jumped into the Milky Way,
Stirred the night and redeemed a dragon.
In Nuo Opera, it shelters the poet who throws himself into
the river.
Before dawn, It returns to its woodcarving,
Wet scales glowed golden lights.

Let the spring breeze go,
Let it spread new things. Let it carve the lion,
In the moonlight let it recite for lays.
Time, the ancient carver —
During the cycle of Beidou's rotation,
Acts as a peace lover, day and night.

19. *A Visit to The Ancient Immortal Cave*

Sir, the medicine is ready. I will
Serve it to the world. The wind,
Is refleshing. The medicine, is turbid.
Nanyang River, and Lingyang River, like two Sensitive poets
Are sobbing with two lines of tears, all the way south,
Into the canister of Taiping Lake.

It will heal my deficiency. When I was young,
I was entangled between the limpitipy and turbidity,(Confused and sober)
Slowly, the rock beneath melted into an ear.
But I come from the state of Chu, and the pomegranate flowers burn my soul.
The bamboo leafs hide sharp edges. All the incomprehension,
Leave it to posterity, just like it be.

The ashram is vast and lush with vanilla. Sir,
Who is the dispenser? -Advance is backward,
The old man on a donkey with back forward. And here,
Prince of Silla built a tower with his flesh.
A sleeping fairy is lying on the win —
He is an expert of chess and a reader of mind.

20. *Visit The Tomb of Tengzijing*

Pine and cypress have left a good reputation. The man who
drew them,
Went to make some tea–
If the people on looking aren't here yet, send to them.
I am like a page boy, galloping
Across the field.
Hands smeared with fresh ink.

Egrets slide over rice seedlings
As a thin layer of snow. Those who pull weeds,
Make that piece of snow fall on top of green bamboos.
Or like a piece of rice paper,
Letting the bamboo bow,
Withstand the forces of stillness.

Who sets the table? Thousands of miles away,
Someone is at the peak of Yueyang Tower,
Flipping through a book make the wind start to blow.
Then, the wind, drank the pot of tea.
While it is blowing,
I slowly open up the ink and wash "Late Autumn of Lake
Dongting".

21. *Pishihang*

My mother was involved in the Pishihang Project. That was before
I came into the world.
"It's bitter, we could only eat a little food a day."
I know nothing about it.

I vowed to go further, like:
Far away, to the Milky Way,
Into the unknown of the universe.
But I never got far. When the moon and the stars are dim,
I always hear the intermittent sound of a river.

People do die. Does the river die?
My mother didn't even know its exact name,
I know it's called the Pi River.
I've never touched it with my skin.
Does it die in my blood?
Or does it never live?

Mother rarely talks about life and death, even though she has arrived
At a precarious age.
I can't imagine a river standing up in a dream,
The dark river will become a white waterfall.
I have never thought that one would lie down alone,
And become a silent river.

22. *Qiangchong*

Are you going to Qiangchong?
Buttercups, milkvetches, purple pansies and impatiens
All remembered you —
You ride the hoops which you rolled as a child
You have gone too far over the clouds. it's time to stop
To get to Qiangchong. Remember to take the short cut,
you kown.

Find a maple tree and a nickname;
Follow the stairs of smoke down;
Find the dark stone in the hearth and question the way.
It'll tell you that it's better to go to Qiangchong
On a winter's night.
Some are talking about their dead relatives by the fire.

It's a place where there's no signal.
Use the roots of plants to navigate.
Year after year, the grass grows, and it shakes hands with
the dead.
It's connected to the umbilical cord you had cut.
It has touched death and been close to life.

Are you going to Qiangchong?
Tonight, you'll be there by moonlight.
At the foot of the hill, the roofs of the poor are whitening.
You will kneel down on your father's grave like a dark
headstone:
No tears of regret,
No proud epitaph.

23. *Flower Stream*

At that moment, the messenger dismounted,
By the banks of the Flower Stream.
Send himself to a floating cloud.
I sat on the shore, and I spoke of my past life,
By the way, I read the letter,
Read it to someone.

Once upon a time, wild flowers were distributed as
Mythical system.
Pebbles used to shine and fly,
If it's a meteorite.
The mountains are like leaves, the sunset is like seals
On the bookmark inscribed "World Peace".

The white clouds returned to the peaks. Thus I finished
reading the letter.
I folded it and hid it in the folds of the river.
Homesickness may dwell in earth's barn,
But history can not.
At the empty ferry, the stream is green.
Back in the old silence, Chang Hong★ was still waiting to
cross.

★Chang Hong(about 565 BC a 492 years ago): He is a famous
scholar, politician, educator and astronomer in ancient
China. He was well versed in mathematics, astronomy and
music. He was famous for his talent, and was once the
teacher of Confucius.

24. *Orchard Maze*

Who will interpret our conversation simultaneously?
- the wind.
It was the first out of the maze.
Who reserved a piece of sunshine
The position for the photo?
— Loquat leaves are clear and clear.

Butterflies stole the show. It's a photographer's
Careless work.
The sunflower spoke out first,
Her point of view
Flowers and seeds in the workshop.
It is true: heaven is much like an orchard.

In the distance, the people who bring water for irrigation,
A poet or a fruit farmer?
From the plank road, the path bifurcated, the nursery
Neat as lines of poetry.
That's his work,
Published in the plain pages.

25. *Sichuan Opera- Face Changing*

He looked for his face in the old papers.
Can he find it? What he found is
Not even his face.
As he searched, he began to wonder,
As if the face,
Is a drag on the body.

The history books has yellowed with age, but every face
Is all brand new
Someone ripped it out page by page, maybe
Only in this way can we understand the histories
As they are. Maybe
Goodlooking faces exist only in legend.

When the music in the background spews out the tongue
of fire,
We couldn't help cheering.
When the applause cools and the lights go out,
He returned to the workshop of the Intangible Heritage Masters.
At that moment, the moon shines in the makeup remover,
And also on his empty face.

26. *Boston Ivy Bar*

When we talked about the lake, temporarily and eternity,
Meet in a watch case.
Willows had drooping needles, and roses
were still ignorant of worldly affairs. They spread to the door,
Which confused people, with confusion.
Egrets stood on one foot to stay alert.

Now, the clouds are coming —
It's like people to the conference are half on their way.
The other half hid in flowers flowers.
Someone is looking through an old book,
In German, <Being and Time>.
The tiny drops of rain try to translate it.

Sparrows never talk, as slugs
Drag out long questions.
In the tick of time, they are reborn as us.
This makes the debate possible-
At night, An absent-minded camphor tree,
Will turn into a lamp.

27. *On The Right Bank of The Yangtze River*

One cannot choose its birthplace,
But can walk along the river bank, and devote the rest of its life
to a spray.
*Zheng He certainly didn't see it that way.
In the cracks of history,
the stars were stable and the sea was raging.

The wind, is blowing through the reeds.
The granary of a nation, cannot be blown.
Agriculture over language,
was achieved modernization earlier.
The force of the river, quietly washed away
The pages of history.

This is the broadest section of the Yangtze River.
— Once a fleet of ships
Lost in legend.
Once the Captain returned to his hometown,
Planting flowers, raising rice seedlings, running marathons.
He chose to grow old on the shore.

*Zheng He: Ming Dynasty eunuch, navigatordiploma. He was sent to the West six times as eunuchs, died on his seventh voyage. Zheng He's voyages to the Western Seas were an unprecedented feat in the world's maritime history in the early 15th century, which played a positive role in the economic and cultural exchanges between China and other countries. He himself is also respected by the vast majority of Chinese people

28. *Pottery*

How do you find fire in pottery? As
Finding the ferry down —
In the cross-section of the Yao River.
Two phoenixes flew out of Siming Mountain.
They were in the fire,
At night.
They completed the firing of legends,
In the raging flames.

In Hemudu site, A realistic tenon
Corresponds a historical mortise.
Time is the purest clay,
Capture the inspiration of black.
Shooting stars, are tumbling from the gabled roof.
They will grow into pearls in black potteries.

The stean is filled with rice, under the stars,
The wellhead is gleaming.
This image has fed us for thousands of years.
As someone growing up by eating rice, I inherited
The hunger of my ancestors.
Referring to the education of the starry sky, I only follow
a half.

29. *Visit Cheng Changgeng Exhibition Hall*

The body is a seven-tiered pagoda. A bird carries a seed, the pagoda
Is added three feet.
Who is singing <The battle in Fancheng> at the top of the tower?
Who's spitting blood,
While embroidering a soul, from a pear flower,
Stitch by stitch , to build the base of the pagota?

My heart is in a tumult. In a hurry,
I painted myself a red face.
Taking off the costume and get naked with reality,
My fate is humble in the dust.
When you played a role as an aged-Sheng in Beijing, with a heavy accent.
I returned with wind and snow, refusing to take a photo with the willows in front of the hall.

The people who are watching the play are actually acting.
The people who act are actually watching it.
Actors go up and down, and in the middle of the stage seated★ Guan Yu; The crowd rejoiced,
The bench was full of★ Cao Cao.
The same mouth, used for cheering, cracking melon seeds,
The same palm, for praying, clapping, and tai chi.

★Guan Yu and Cao Cao are Characters in beijing opera

30. *Ancient Pottery of Doumu*

Time gave me a broken clay pot. Placed in the corner,
It fed
A blade of mugwort, with a few drops of rain.
Neem had lost its leaves and began to lose its fruits.
The rest of time,
is taken over by small talks. Remaining earth is boiling in
raging flames.

I hear the cry of a piece of pottery.
— an incense burner,
Doesn't want to salt and pickle potherb mustard. The broken
do not want to be whole.
They can't decide anything.
Birds flying from a jar to a telephone pole, Their droppings
Carve for it as a souvenir.

Flower arrangers love broken pots,
I love crushing
Thin ice in an earthenware jar. The dragon kiln makes the
backbone of the earth,
Sometimes a dragon is made, too. Thousands of miles of land,
Riches in setaria, as art binding.
Red bricks are mottled, wooden doors are unlatched,
sunlight is glazing our shadows.

31. *Discuss Nonfiction with My Deskmate*

Speaking of fiction, snowflakes
Covered Tianzhu Mountain.
Speaking of nonfiction, be a fish. In the ruts, in the abyss,
Bite into
Phenomenon of the fish hook. Speaking of that sentence,
The mountains are playing a soft harmonica, with the sound
of a thousand folds.

★I have the gaze of the abyss and you
have the tiredness of a tortuous journey.
How real life is, taking words out of glowing red coals, steaming.
★A crucian carp,
Is waiting for the water of the Xijiang River,
Is this fiction or non-fiction?

Believe in what we present on paper.
Believed that his friend, who had died of a chronic illness,
was inside the top-
Rotation. No one could save him.
When we give the words to the snow,
Just like our conversation,
Deep and futile. Dawn never visited us before the snow melted.

★It cite from <Thus Spake Zarathustra> writer by Friedrich
Wilhelm Nietzsche "When you gaze into an abyss, be
careful, for the abyss gazes into you."
★"A crucian carp, is waiting for the water of the Xijiang
River. "This is from literary quotation of Zhangzi, Which
refers to fake friendship.

32. *Listen to Dai Rui Reciting Yueyang Tower*

Like thunder into the moon cleaning arms.
For a long time, no one used rafter pens,
Quietly sweep the fine snow from the yard.
I remember in 2014, someone sent a book with a letter inside:
Jufei, has not been back to Anhui for more than half a year.
I don't know when you'll be back.

Now I am walking on the snowy mountain road,
Catching a dilemma.
My father, carrying a load of tofu,
Frost on his temples. Who can back with me?
My father, has died in the winter of 2017.
That night, In the southeast of Anhui bright moon trinidad.

We'll eat it together next spring,
The gift of the Dabie Mountains–
And how many temples were destroyed by meteorites in dreams?
The repairs I made,
Were resowinging a square of chrysanthemums in front of the court.
The practice I did,
Was to relifing a meteor softly , free in the Milky Way.

33. *Chalk Snow Maker*

Follow the footprints to find someone? Spring
Is gonna cut you off in front of us.
Down the fireworks of pigeons? Snow, maybe
Tear down the language barrier for you
The lake is bidding farewell, the ridge is retreating,
Bamboo has a heavy body.

The wind, more and more specific, while the scenery
Become abstract. This is the time to be an ancient person.
The moonlight is spreading and cold, and ruts
Are drawing parallel lines. From the very beginning, You
never should have
Into the maze of snow. From the very beginning,
You shouldn't miss the chalk snowmaker.

Dug up spinach buried in the snow. Chip away
The snow lasting ten years. "The snow is falling tightly."
How many times you have dreamed of backing to the class.
Still in explaining the word "tightly".
All fell into silence, all beings held their breath,
A quiet, tiny snow fell.

34. *Drink in Snow Weather*

Friends from Hangzhou sent Shaoxing wine, also planning
To sent me the snow of Lake Pavilion.
And what makes snow unique is its unreality,
All these, let the tipsy snow
Become a reality. We were toasting, in the video
There are pieces of snow, outside in the sky.

Forgive the futility of middle age, like forgive
A snowman melts after the weather is fine.
Forgive the snowman for being bloated, hypocritical, and
vulnerable,
Like forgiving yourself
But we are still like hyaline, sharp ice,
The fire of life is roasting us.

Snow never speaks up for itself, instead it cures wound
For the river bank. There used to be a Chinese tallow tree,
Sold to a tree dealer in the winter. So many old stories, so
many old friends, only
The snow is new. "Snowflakes fell on every street, for
thousands of times"
Which one hides our years of pain?

35. *A Snow-Falling Sunset*

The snow fell on the wild duck and hid its darkness.
Wild ducks fell on the lake,
A dash of time, presented
The flatness of the world.
The snow on the road has was cleared,
But the snow on the lake is reasonable.

How we loved, the irrationality part of the world,
When we were young.
At dusk, thin snow, covered pigeon droppings.
One piece of snow chased another.
The mountains are straight and cold,
Stretching white to the flat earth.

Picking the snow off the bottom of your boot is like abandoning
The ring of lies.
Who doesn't love coriander, leeks and winter bamboo shoots?
We heading into the kitchen,
Want to waste my life here
Wintersweet open in the snow, well versed in the meaning
of existence.

36. *The Songs of Porcelain*

An egret flits along the river in the early morning.
Like Music played by porcelain
A delayed note.
Music compensated for the lack of celadon.
And those who hit the vase,
Is an ascetic monk in a previous life.

— His walking stick
Root of a sheath used for questioning.
The woman playing the bell, put
An empty bowl on the head.
An egret flying out of an empty bowl must be three more than
That flew into xiqin:

One has been described in the preceding paragraph and will
not be repeated.
One collects thunder, drizzle, and stomach bugs,
From one to a group.
Another, perched on the eaves of the temple,
Overlooking the arm wrestling determination
Between wild chrysanthemum and stone.

37. *At The Bank of Fang Jia River*

In ancient times, A Chinese toon lived eight thousand years
old and still young
The moment the fine stones swing across the stream.
It's the same hands.
Picking waxberry, and making electric soldering iron.
And the peasant woman returned empty-handed from the
back hills,
My lines felt guilty for her sackful of fallen leaves.

The slate is as flat as stele of Wei. Time is broken,
A dog bark as a punctuation mark
Never coming out of a cage.
Lost people to ask the way to ginkgo, ancient camphor
Speak for it. The bookman found the old pawn shop,
To trade fame for youth.

Everything is still, except
The slogan on the wall.
"Anything but self-confession" ★.
The windmill whirled under the eaves. On the roof,
A blob of ink,
To color the universe.

★ Milosh's verse.

38. *Mountains in Emerald Color*

The wind stirred the lake. The celadon of this lake,
Is enough for heaven.
And the hand does not need large objects,
Sight and heart do.
— In the cracks of history,
The sea is blue， and he has half of it.

Misty drizzle, white cranes lightly fell on the ancient town.
It was to be made into a pattern of porcelain,
And its cry
Will be an inscription. At the museum, as we talked,
A crane flying out of the language,
Transformed into a bird whistle of Wei and Jin dynasties.

The dragon kilns laid in the mountains,
How many green dragons have you made? Now I got one,
in the poem
Looming and looming.
Under the ink, everything but me was a complete sagger.
A thousand peaks and my verses,
Are both broken jade of heaven and earth.

39. *Bridge South Street*

Those who do not speak in the uncultivated land are not
limited to language
But by "speaking out" —
Bees come to his rescue, wings reveal the secrets of the sun
There's a stone vat， in front of the door。
There were a couple of duckweeds, like a tight-lipped person
In those stormy nights.

It was not Cai Xiang who wrote "Practice in early morning
upon a rooster begin to crow" on the lintel.
But by a man send back white clouds from Southeast Asia
His daughter is swarthy, under the wiliers
Washing the oysters. The sea breeze is blowing, she is so
happy a girl
As if the sky above the red brick house
Is cleaned by her, too.

I took a picture in front of the stone carvings of "Peace
forever"
A gull skimmed the spindrift, and flew into the mangrove
I saw myself coming towards me, on Luoyang Bridge
Once and once again—
One came from Ceylon, smelling of seaweed
One backed from thousands of miles away, holding
yellowing map.

40. *Griefs and Joys — to Li Shutong*

Is the cypress outside the door, bankrupt?
I'll see you later.
From the "I", Xu Huanyuan escaped,
And did not enter the memorial hall under construction.
That year, it snowed heavily in old Shanghai. Today,
A dead tree seems to be singing: after we were apart, even
the dreams Were cold and empty.

Beside bodhi, and magnolia grandiflora, young mother is
Holding her leaping daughter.
Leaves, blue sky, gold coins of sunshine,
Are the Lotus Ashram, and also dripping with blood.
He that deserts his wife and children is merciful, I believe it
Or not: Mercy to the world, why do you only hurt me?

Boy playing top, had homed for dinner.
On the banyan tree, a hanging beard was to sent to Japan.
The sun was over the western hill, and the frosty was on
grasses,
Magpie bit pine branches, the playboy became a monk.
The world of mortals is rolling, and the incense is curling.
One is at the broken bridge, the other is at the corner of
the earth.

41. Overlooking Xian Gong Mountain in The Distance

Look up: I was getting along well with clouds. After saying goodbye, Years later,
we ran into each other again
Blue sky has unrealistic blue, I have
The possibility of rational flight
Where does Fairy Live? In the deepest blue, ordinary
Two bedrooms and one living room. He's paying off his mortgage

Look ahead: Mountains vying with one another, want to
Go to the sea.
A Chinese fir, breaking the root and rising, wants to occupy the sky
A bird, flies away and back.
It landed on the Sky Pavilion. A crowd pouring up onto the Rice Rock
Wanted a drink of the fountain of Greed

Majia Town at the foot of the mountain, are rising cooking smoke. Village Women, finish cooking
To fix the reservoir,
Or go to the beach and wait for her husband.
If she asks for divination, I'll let her wait
When the moon is clear and the stars are sparse, shipwrecks from the deep will come
A voice or two of the Southern Opera

42. *Tiger in My Heart*

In the absence of tigers, they are in my heart —
A dewdrop hunging on the tip of grass, and in the slow rolling light,
Contains a tiger's lighting cut and pounce.
Are you willing to feed a tiger with your flesh? Are you willing to be under
The ruler of the stars, and bury the Whistle Stick
Under the pine trees of Jingyang Hillock?

How many fires kindle the autumn,
To be part of the tiger fighting team,
One of the colorful. How much wine I should drink,
To free the tiger, or to transform the Yellow River Delta,
To a flying tiger flag. The tiger made a jolt in the sun, its roar is
If not silent, It will penetrate the mountains and rivers.

I am one of the generation of grass eaters who grind their teeth.
Inside me, the gully torn by the hungry tiger,
Can't be plant a single lotus stump; and by the side,
Not even a kingfisher with a hanging eye.
The drumsticks of Salt Mound break the cage of autumn,
I followed the beat and put out my front paws.

43. *A Section of The Yellow River, and to Jiang Yiwei*

The river was as quiet as the setting sun. It's the very Yellow
river,
That's how it should be. I should make my way through
the crowd,
Commit myself to1
A patch of grass. I should walk faster on the pontoon.
I should jump into the river, but shouldn't wash myself —
I'm too clear,
Transparent blood vessels, can not find the inheritance of
mother tongue.

I should have taken a sip of the water. And follow the
following sand and mud,
Let the sand in my stomach replace the dust in my dreams.
Ask the doctor who did the chest X-ray,
Look at my rough, muddy, and broken part.
Be a man who doesn't need a ferry,
Go straight to the sea and disappear.

When there is no way, it is time to seize the way.
Down from the high dike,
In the face of burning water, Just as lonely
As the moth of truth. This little stretch of the Yellow River,
The four of us should take a picture together. The Weihe
River and the Pishe Rivers,
As well as a drop of water from the Wei river and The
Fujiang River should be returned to the sea.★

*Weihe River, Pishe River, Wei River and Fujiang river are the mother rivers of Dingxi, Gansu province, Lu 'an, Anhui Province, Xinxiang, Henan Province and Suining, Sichuan Province respectively, which belongs to the four friends' hometown.

44. *Under The Starry Sky*

When there are few people, the stars are clear.
The stars were low
God instantly lit it up
The lights of another country.
As a low-flying prodigal son, I smell
The smell of cow dung in a bootes' smoke.

Who sang a song
The ballad of captivity?
Under the stars, a free singer
Is coming from the cottonwood.
If he was an oil worker,
Please let me call you brother.

The Yellow River is ten miles away,
She doesn't speak.
The autumn wind is a hundred miles away and she doesn't
speak.
The stars, thousands of miles away,
Separate a shooting star
Into the black hole of language.

45. *Silkworms Have Their Own Motherland*

So is autumn. In Linjia Village, Longju Town,
So is a cloud.
So are the short spikes on the flower drum.
So does the silkworm woman's watch over the white cocoon.
Their respective countries together,
Are also my country.

Is there anything broader?
Mulberry forest ripples, not as yellow as the Yellow River.
A red dragonfly landed on
Flat mulberry Leaf airport.
The rustle of the silkworm room
Is a storm of a young man's memories.

... Father's hair grew grey overnight, spitting out long silk.
The cocoons on the straw look like moonlight
Fuzzy and cold. From the Dabie Mountains to the Yellow
River estuary,
He went from losing his father to becoming one.
From being trapped in his own cocoon to emerging from it,
Soaring in the sky over his wider motherland.

46. *Home*

I choose my return flight
Near the porthole,
Not just to get close to the sky. I'd like to have a look at it,
A big river on a scroll in the field,
How to pour into the sea.
With the style of running script.

Under the clouds, a ship was towing
Long white ripples. Like a plow cow,
Plow the rich field.
I believe the men on board now looked up,
Watching planes fly across the sky,
It's the same metaphor.

Where yellow meets blue, a big river
Like a wandering wanderer,
She threw herself into her mother's arms.
After years of dust,
After suffering, a new life was obtained.
Sobbing, also happy —

47. *Rouge Button*

Rain wet bleak tired.
Never arrive,
Just — disappear in transit.
Silence that floats on flowers,
Emptiness that goes into a cup.

I wish I were black characters on white papers,
But this is far from true.
I would be the knife, I would be the ink.
I wish invisible things could be touched:
The early spring in the forecast, the girl after the filter.
Rain in solemn rain boots.

Not once have I,
Violated your smooth flesh.
In dreams,
When you present the fragrance in your body, The path I open,
It's not worth mentioning.

48. *One Night at Dongying*

I can describe my dreams:
A coin was picked up on the forked path.
I met a manger when I was lost.
For the same sin, under the low eaves
I can't stand up straight; Because of speaking in accent,
I'm like your poor relatives.

The house has not yet been built,
Autumn is coming.
No trial, but humiliation.
Someone said in a humble voice,
There is leftover for the hungry and water
To the thirsty......

Finally, the moon set. The autumn wind heard
The sound of ginkgo turning yellow.
A novel that he has read,
Invented the solitude of the north–
There is no wind and waves in Bohai Bay,
The night was dark and quiet.

49. *A Night in Li Zhuang*

Under the stone wall of tongji Middle School's playground,
he read:
The ashes of Mr. So-and-so,
It's 200 meters straight ahead in the middle of the river.
At night, the whistle comes, like a long bell at the end of a class.
The tombstones carved on the embankment,
Rubbed lightly by the eraser of the moon.

You came down from the river,
Like a pear flower to the rosy clouds. Like an egret, to the
branches of darkness.
You consume each other, in a long conversation.
It seems that the whetstone licks the blade.
Faraway town,
You changed his life with a piece of chalk.

From midnight until dawn he let himself go through the
clumps of wormwood.
Through the salt of the world, through the snow of the palm,
Wet his shoes by the river,
Wait for the stars to disperse, with a stone heart.
And what does the river say,
No one knows. Wood latticed Windows, seeping into the
morning light.

50. *Listen to The Rain at Dongpu Reservoir*

When the first rain broke the mirror of the reeds,
My heart quivered. Like a silver fish,
Getting rid of all the dirty parts of my soul.
Heaven and earth have their modernity, and the lake,
Is timeless classicism, for example
In the rain, there is a blank, there is chaos.
But this is for listening to the rain, not watching the rain,
Let's just close our eyes and unscrew
Faucets of history, Let reality hand over hearing aids.
I thought of the girl who did the intelligent speech research,
She's gonna be on the audio I sent,
Who can hear the level and oblique tone of sycamore leaves
on science island.

51. *Autumn Scenery of Shushan - to Gao Zheng*

A good friend of me, is a floating cloud; on good terms
with you,
They are dialectic jagged rocks. A shoe cuts his foot,
He can still walk fast when climbing mountains.
It's a pointer, a spinning top that you whip.
It's the eraser I'm holding, the sweat drops
Like a swirl of chalk dust.
But koelreuteria is our common relative, and when autumn
comes,
Her crown is waiting to be claimed by us pupils.
Two egrets flew up into her crown, become two
Indistinct pearls. Fallen leaves for you, and for me,
The addressee's address was a pine-needle alley,
And it is also a branch for homesick.
Night wind is a qualified postman, ant
It's a smart regular script. As one nears middle age,
What matters about a name?
Even we walked across step by step, not a footprint left,
except bluestone steps;
No more than an array of wild goose,
That disappears over the TV tower in a blue of wideness.

52. *From Kuang River to Swan Lake*

The autumn wind is trying to persuade me, as well as
swallows, plum trees and rocks.
Everything can be persuaded to be part of a partnership,
All things in motion abolish prejudice.
The man was lit up by the river in spring, now the sunset
of autumn
Is shining on his face. Oh, his face,
Is as holy as the surface of Swan Lake.
He wants to be alone, leaving him a camphor forest —
Camphor fruit fell all over the ground, stepped on, there is
a faint thunder.
He didn't have to climb to the top of the camphor tree
To receive the education of autumn wind.
If you want to get together, give him a tunnel,
Cross the floor of Swan Lake and meet the autumn wind again

53. *The Wulidun Overpass*

On the way to Hefei, it is necessary to pass through
Wulidun overpass. Many a morning,
I hurried past, like an impatient boy
Many a night,
I walked slowly, with plenty of patience.
I even walked under the bridge once —
Ivy and oleander, trying to block my way home.
Two or three couples, a few walkers
Seniors, walking in the dusk,
With a golden hue on their face,
Are a group of moving icons. And I am the only pilgrim.

54. *Good Night, Changjiang West Road*

Good night, study boy. Good night
A river with gold code
Written all over it. Good night, artificial intelligence invisibility.
Good night, you engineer holds a hub in the library,
Reading Zhuangzi Additional Chapters —
The clouds have emotionally reserved
Hot towel for you. Good night Wanxiang Town,
Good night Chinese Shopping Center, Good night the
tickling sound of credit cards.
Good night, you are waving goodbye, I will see you again
Overpass. Good night, old professor of Sound Valley.
He is fighting to himself in the blueprints show, and then
An inverted spider accompanies him.
Good night camphor, how many years have l waited in line.
Killing dragons, or riding the tigers, to become a road.
Good night magnolia, and street light form intertext.
Good night, utopia on the sand table,
The ancient moon lits mountaineers.

55. *A Whistle*

In the morning, open the window, push away
the residual snow and bird song.
So much bad news, and the bird doesn't know it.
Last night, a cold wind blew snow,
Like a god whistling between heaven and earth.
After dawn, the fields were a vast expanse of white,
As if nothing had happened.

56. *Spring Fair*

In the afternoon, A mower tore through the grass and saw
A toad did not move.
Inside it, a little sami
Arguing with elms and hungry tigers —
It's is sunny and the mountains and rivers are pretty, suitable
for funeral.
The spring breeze is busy in site clearing,
And cooking smoke has to reverse.
The chimney stands up straight,
Awaiting sentencing. There is no bitterness in his heart.
Mowing is optional,
But the mower is still alive. His baske
is full of thatchthes,
And time is still empty.
Tractors is pushing spring and grey birds on trees
Is coming back one by one.
The idle wicker is dark green.
Never mind, All of these things.

57. *I Never Found Myself*

last night, he was chopping wood and carrying water in the temple,
And studied dragon bending. This morning at the meeting,
His slides wouldn't open,
And chrysanthemums are full of thermos.
Inside the punch machine, there's an abstract version of him
So, Where is the specific he?
In the drizzle of the little school,
Or in the textbook with the cover torn off?
In the mystery of cicada slough,
Or beneath a towering reservoir dam?
(Oh, he was worried it might suddenly crash.)
In the clatter of the paddle scratching the water,
Or at an empty levee?
In the cry of the dry riverbed, or in a letter
To time?

58. *Being and Time*

I have an alarm clock, which refuses to move;
I have a walnut, it is young.

I went to a funeral when I was eight,
Lively atmosphere
Makes me want to die too.
When my poor relative died,
Clutching a discarded pendulum.

Her hands used to grow vegetables,
Now is holding her own time.
Her face, wrinkled like a walnut,
Is a clock that will never work.

59. *Orders of Late Autumn*

A group of pines and cypresses are running on the hill
The way they lean, the fire under their feet
They carry the wind of the years
Their forgetfulness of the past, and their secrects
Are secrets
I have to speed up, to see what is happening
I must give up the green of life
To reach the warmness of burning

I have long cherished the memory of a man who chopped
wood for winter
He breathed, in the sun
His love to peaceful life
Makes me feel guilty. He was dressed little
Split a running tree in two, how fast
He sat up, cut off the fall, how vast

60. *Longzi Lake*

Embrace the moon and bury it at the bottom of the lake.
From now on,
There is one less angry man on the street.

Fish leaped out and the lake rippled.
The light shines in the place
Where the moon shone last year.
Only moonlight can arrive and clean.

I am used to collecting cones under a pine tree
And surrender my heart of Song Dynasty, in an ancient building

But the autumn wind does not know
Whose song is fair-sounding, on the mountain road.
I was addicted to it and became a water ghost.

I slip out of the noisy crowd
Gazing at the lake, desperation captures me

The mud at the bottom of the lake, hides a sky map
There is only one moon, in the middle of the sky

61. *A Sleepwalker*

Mirrors in dreams spread their wings.
On the beach, there are jars of time.

The unpredictable, ever-changing
Stones are in the belly of the river.

He, has been standing there for a long time.
Like criminals on the verge of death, waiting for the
punishment of the setting sun.

He tells the stranger who he is.
He has no weight. He's empty.

62. *En Attendant Godot*

The weather forecast says it will rain tomorrow.
Rain will come from Qiang Chong,
Fall into the afternoon nap station.
Why should I be an outcast?
In the office building,
I wait to spit the sand out of my mouth.

Eight o'clock in the evening,
The provincial courier returns to the rental house, horses inside
Burst out of the red overalls.
Lettuce waits in the kitchen for the blade of a kitchen knife.
The adventure games it loves,
Is rolling in the iron pot of life.

Tell the turdus merula and sparrow. It's easy to find the lost
temple,
If holding a torch.
Hidden scheming,
We can make a deal at Starbucks.
If we go to Shaoyaoju by carriage,
The messenger will not disappear into the subway.

63. *Playing Chess by The Roadside*

After work, many pieces reveal their true shapes。
They talked about the stock market and palace dramas。
Under the buttonwood tree where he was decapitated,
The two men fought to the death.

The middle-aged man stood with a cigarette in his left hand.
His minister was dead,
Buried in the separated field in Pengcheng City.
But he still had a black horse, leaping across the board.
By the Chu River, someone sings —
"Look at the King sleeping in his tent with his clothes on."

An old man sat down at the other end.
His Rooks was lost and his Cannons failed to fire.
The King with no accompany is very idle, back to his
replacement building,
He paced back and forth, collecting the rent.

Spring had not yet arrived in the west of Hua Jia field
A pawn, took the bullet train and crossed the Han border.

64. *Homesickness at Sunset — to Li Jie*

Boozers: Goodbye. Just you and me, practice
Spiraling upward. When we reach the fifth floor, The years emerge
The verse of our memory. This is the same as the Yellow Crane Tower
How different! No wood, pine cones
No memorial arch, bathed in bells. No giant pen
Write out "The mountains and rivers are magnificent and picturesque."! Where there is grass, there is a skyscraper
The old friend who resigned from the west, without saying a word, blocked the circle of friends
There were yellow cranes, but they were far away. There's the Yangtze River, and it doesn't just flow at farewell time;
But my hometown, still far away, still have to transfer from high-speed rail to light boat
Floating down the river, crossing layers of loess, sitting in the Ruins of Yin and crying...
On the ferry, this realistic fireworks to the romantic section
We talked about the gun at the memorial, the moment the revolution started
How similar its heat and sweetness was to the weather before us
Talking about the drinker at the table, yellow sand, iron boat, small arrow, because of this verse
They left a pen name. And their real names just dissipated...
I want to go to the temple as you want to go to the top
Do you see a sail when you look far into the world of Chu? No.
I do like incense offerings, on my tortoise shell

Destined to be stamped with Chinese — it's a bronze crane
Wings that can fly. In the square, lotus flowers are in full bloom
Acacia leaves comb the heat. Your hand
Stuck with indelible chalk dust, I don't care of standing in the mud
Dragging my tail. I am looking for the source of this mysterious Chinese language
Where does it come from, in the middle of the river, in a building
Blooming flowers of language. It's part of what you and I do
It is the sound of a book read, a magnificent white cloud
Years from now, when your successor inherits your job, he stands at the podium
Will he grind this poem into gravel? Would he Tear this building down
Into vermillion lacquer, glazed tile, rafters and cement bricks?

65. *Records of Visit to Tushan*

A drop of water at the point of The White Horse Mountain,
has come so far
Before he saw the Huai River. If down, through the dust
of history
It will be governed on a sacrificial vessel filled with fire
It was autumn, and the river was still
On the harvest of grain, the village rang out intoxicating
Flowerdrum Opera
Last night's meteor, hiding in Longzi Lake
Told us a secret
Don't speak loudly when climbing mountains
Do not hide in a pine tree
Bewitched by the Nine-tailed Spirit Fox, he easily handed
over the key to wisdom
Princes in assembly, wives -pregnants
Rather than building an ark,
Lead the stream of desire to the sea
When climbing the mountain, I saw huge stones split by swords
Used to waiting for thousands of years
Jing Moutain on the other side is silent like a persimmon tree
Roadside wild chrysanthemum, also do not say a word
Sitting on the steps, mountain wind blowing through me,
also blowing the legend★ to me:
The baby cries in the cradle,
His father had just passed the door.

★In ancient times, the Great Yu,busy in governing the
Yellow River, chose not to enter his house, even if he had
three chances to go home to see his wife and kids.

66. *Riddle*

I want to release a yellow crane and leave myself empty
It carries water from the Yangtze River
To moisten the birch's eyes, to wash
Pigeon droppings from the old castle. It trades water from
the Yangtze River
To the water of the Orca River, let me watering orchids in
the morning
on Snake Mountain. Buzzing bees,
It has only one thorn that keeps me
Deepen my love on life.

Replace the Yangtze River bridge in front of you with a
volume of scriptures from Tang and Song dynasties

Set the clock back; I'm going to be late
To the south. The setting sun shattered over the river
In your deep blue eyes,
There are fading evenings
And fate is always a riddle, vertigo.

Printed in the United States
by Baker & Taylor Publisher Services